DANIEL W. EVANS

YOUR TIME

The Greatest Gift
You Receive and Give

Your Time

The Greatest Gift You Receive and Give

Daniel W. Evans

2023© by Daniel W. Evans

BIBLE SCRIPTURES

Printed in the United States of America by

SPIRIT MEDIA

spiritmedia.us

Spirit Media and our logos are trademarks of

Spirit Media
1249 Kildaire Farm Rd STE 112
Cary, NC 27511
1 (888) 800-3744

Books › Business & Money › Skills

Paperback ISBN: 978-1-961614-04-8
Hardback ISBN: 978-1-958304-69-3
Audiobook ISBN: 978-1-958304-71-6
eBook ISBN: 978-1-958304-70-9
Library of Congress Control Number:
2023902959

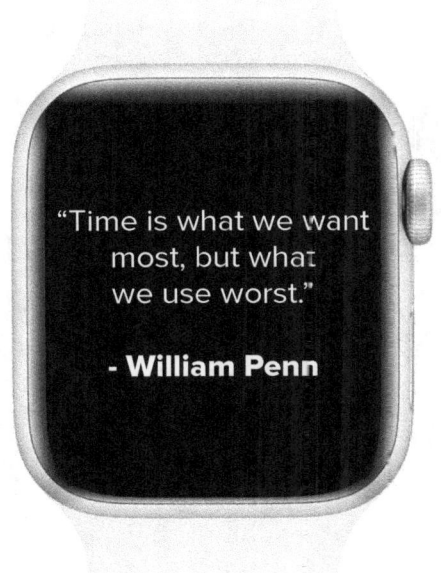

CONTENTS

"My favorite things in life don't cost any money. It's really clear that the most precious resource we all have is time."

- Steve Jobs

Think about a song from the '60s titled *Time Is on My Side*, by the Rolling Stones. In no way does the song insinuate that humankind has any control of time. Every movement of the second hand on the clock brings us closer to eternity. There is no stopping it. It is as sure as the law of gravity, which is universal.

God is an eternal being and He set time in motion for the earth.

The Bible says in **2 Peter 3:8 (NIV)**, "... With the Lord a day is like a thousand years, and a thousand years are like a day." This is in reference to time on earth as compared to eternity.

Isaiah 38:8 (AMPC) says, "Behold, I will turn the shadow [denoting the time of day] on the steps or degrees, which has gone down on the steps or sundial of Ahaz, backward ten steps or degrees. And the sunlight turned back ten steps on the steps on which it had gone down."

God turned time backward ten degrees because Hezekiah requested it. There are several theories attempting to explain this unnatural movement of sunlight that affected time. We need to be careful, because attempting to explain what happened can lead some to questioning and doubting God and the supernatural.

It is good that science can substantiate biblical facts. However, we need to acknowledge that faith requires no explanation.

TAKE A MOMENT TO FOCUS

---

*Read the question and
write what comes to mind.*

Do you have faith that God can help you with your time, even in supernatural ways?

_____

_____

_____

_____

_____

_____

_____

_____

_____

_____

_____

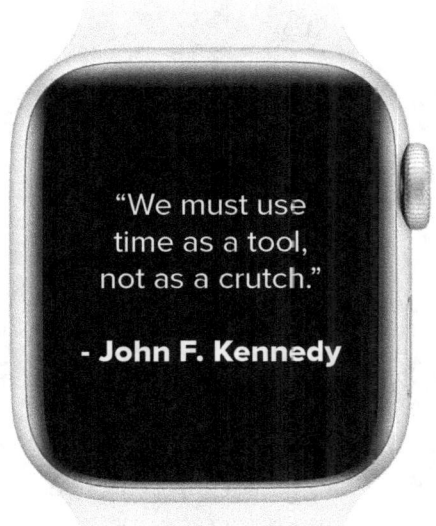

"We must use
time as a tool,
not as a crutch."

- John F. Kennedy

The sundial is a timepiece referred to in scripture. However, historically there were other means of measuring time, as well. Even during the night watches of old, there had to be a means of measuring hours.

Time devices were invented for the purpose of monitoring and managing time. We monitor time by increments from millennia, centuries, decades, years, months, weeks, days, hours, minutes, seconds, to milliseconds. We even measure the speed of light in light years.

We monitor and manage our lives by using calendars and clocks. We set appointments, leave for work and school, lie down, wake up, and plan vacations and holidays. We eat meals, spend time with family, and attend church by using the measuring tools of time. Daily, we schedule many other tasks using these tools, as well.

Even our goal-setting is marked on calendars—whether on our devices or on paper. We plan days, weeks, months, and even years into our futures. And our tools, such as calendars, are very important to our success.

In the end, though, man cannot control time or change it. All we can do is monitor it and trust God to give us the time we attempt to manage each and every day.

TAKE A MOMENT TO FOCUS

*Read the question and
write what comes to mind.*

Do you trust God with your future,
even if it is scheduled?

_____

_____

_____

_____

_____

_____

_____

_____

_____

_____

_____

"You may delay,
but time will not."

- Benjamin Franklin

We are the best managers of our own time. No one can manage our own personal time as well as each of us—and we still have trouble. Not even our own family members know every little detail of our life throughout the day. If you really think about it, who will want to? Face a fact! Each one of us has trouble managing our own time.

Unforeseen situations can bombard us on any given day. Whether at work, school, home, church, traveling, or even in the dentist's chair, there are unknowns that present themselves. The dentist may say, "Uh oh, cavity!" And there you are now, spending time dealing with the cavity you did not plan for. Or how about a flat tire? Or, God forbid, a health issue, or an emergency with a family member or friend?

The point here is, we work hard at managing our time every day. Then we attempt to fit God, family, and others into it. Yet, perhaps we need to adjust our priorities instead of tacking God on at the end of our to-do list. Because news flash! We would be well served to plan everything else around the most important things: God, family, and others.

Some may say, "There is hardly enough time for the daily routine, much less those important things." Therefore, managing time is vital. Everyone will manage time around his or her most important priorities.

Daniel took time to pray daily, even with threats of being cast into a den of lions **(Daniel 6)**. You may be obstinate and proclaim sternly, "Yeah, but people did cast him among hungry lions." Yes, they did. But no harm came to him—and he prospered in the kingdom. There are always rewards attached to prioritizing properly.

Yet, all of us can be honest about the fact that, oftentimes, we need to check our priorities. While family, friends, and circumstances may force themselves upon us, God will not. The top priority in our time management to-do list must be to give Him time each day. Remember, He does not operate in time, but He does control time. This leads us back to trusting Him, because we constantly need assistance with managing our own time.

TAKE A MOMENT TO FOCUS

*Read the question and
write what comes to mind.*

Is God included in your daily routines
of managing your schedules?

_____

_____

_____

_____

_____

_____

_____

_____

_____

_____

_____

_____

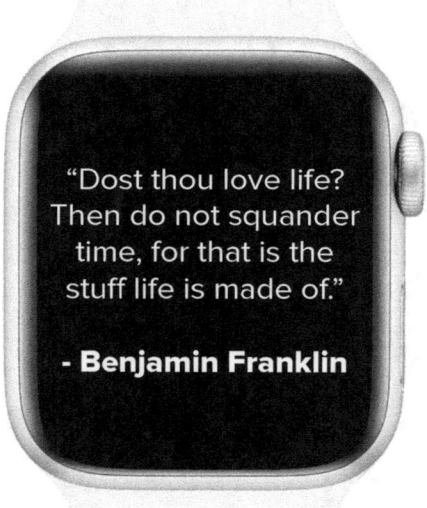

"Dost thou love life?
Then do not squander
time, for that is the
stuff life is made of."

- Benjamin Franklin

Many times, we clearly see, God and the things of God are not properly prioritized as they should be, and we suffer spiritually for it. We even suffer in other ways because of it. My prayer is that this booklet will help you recognize and realize that you are a potential success. And you can achieve success by becoming aware of the value of your time.

Hopefully, by the time you reach the last of these pages, you can honestly say that you need to check your priorities, because, remember, God will not force Himself on us. The Holy Spirit is constantly at work speaking to our hearts about what God desires to do in us. His desire is to take us to new heights in Him. With this in mind, we need to take the time to listen and obey.

The top priority in managing time is to give God some of ours every day. Remember, God does not operate in time, but He does control it. It is not that He needs time with us. The fact is that we need time with Him. This leads us back to an earlier statement about trusting Him, because we constantly need assistance with managing our own time. It makes sense to allow the One that can help us manage time to take part in something so important.

Time is precious. We cannot replace it. In addition, no matter how hard we try, we cannot move time backward or manipulate it in any way. We have a certain allotment of time. Therefore, we must manage it and spend it well.

The Bible says we all have an appointment with death **(Hebrews 9:27)**. Correspondingly, David asks the Lord to help him know his end and the measure of his days **(Psalm 39:4)**.

The bottom line: our time on earth is limited and God is the only one who knows how much we have. He must be the priority in our lives since He knows how much time we have. Working together with Him will clearly help us be better managers of our time.

TAKE A MOMENT TO FOCUS

---

*Read the question and
write what comes to mind.*

Do you acknowledge how much you need God and then realize how much more time you need with Him?

_____

_____

_____

_____

_____

_____

_____

_____

_____

_____

"Make use of t'me,
let not advantage
slip..."

- William Shakespeare

There is a part of time management that we easily overlook, and which robs us of many blessings. It is the giving of our time.

Just as we must prioritize our time around God, we must give some of our time to others. You may be questioning, "My life will drastically change just by prioritizing time for God, and now I have to include others?" "Really?"

Yes. God cares very much for people, which is why He sent His Son to die on the cross! If we are to be Christ-like, we must do as Christ did. He fit people into His schedule everywhere He went.

When Jesus was on the way to Jerusalem, He stopped and took time to bless babies and little children **(Luke 18:15-17)**. Even with the disciples' efforts to hold back the children, Jesus took the time.

Are our schedules so tight that we cannot stop for a divine appointment? This question is one to take seriously, especially when we are prompted to do so by the Holy Spirit. The appointment could be simply scheduling a visit with someone, helping someone, or making a phone call.

Cornelius made the time to obey God and send for Peter **(Acts 10)**. He did not check his schedule or put it off. He learned that when God speaks, we must make time to listen and then take the time to obey. Remember the following reasons why God speaks to us. When He speaks and asks us to do something, it is for one of two reasons. The first is to get us to a point of being a blessing to someone else, or secondly, for us to receive a blessing. It was Cornelius' time to receive just such a blessing.

Cornelius also made the time to visit his family and friends. He invited them to come to his house to hear the words of Peter. There is another side to this coin of giving time, as Acts illustrates. Peter made the time to invite the men Cornelius sent to stay overnight, even against his religious indoctrination. He then followed them the next day to Cornelius' house, which was also against the Jews' religious customs.

These are the positions God desires for all of us to take. We may not be one of those people who are able to travel spontaneously as Peter did. However, we may be able to visit as Cornelius did, with a little planning and time.

In fact, we must always remember to prioritize and plan to do what pleases God. And one of the greatest ways to please Him is by helping others. If we are honest with ourselves, we can spare some time to do a good deed.

Once again, time is valuable—an absolutely irreplaceable asset. Therefore, invest it well! Unlike wasted money that may be replaceable, we only have one shot at time.

TAKE A MOMENT TO FOCUS

*Read the question and
write what comes to mind.*

Considering how much time Jesus spent ministering to people, are you spending enough time with the family, friends and others?

_____

_____

_____

_____

_____

_____

_____

_____

_____

_____

"There are no secrets
that time does
not reveal."

- Jean Racine

Many churchgoers think that church is the best or only place to give of their time. In addition, many believe that if they give of their time at church, they fulfill their time investment quota.

In validated national statistics, a high percentage of Christians report that they do not tell others about Christ. In the same study, respondents reveal that the number of visits they make to the sick or those in prison is low.

When I travelled as an evangelist though the states, I listened to many pastors talk about church growth. I noted that when church attendees are absent for a time, they oftentimes are not called to see how they are doing. Neither is there follow-up on new attendees. So again, although working at a church is good, it is not the only way to invest time into people. Perhaps there is a whole world out there that isn't reaping the proper time investment from those in the church.

Recently, I have taken the average attendance of my home church, Living Waters Christian Community in Durham NC, and made a list of every volunteer worker. I calculated the average percentage of workers that give of their time to be 36 percent. This is a much, much higher number than what I have read the national average to be.

Even my church's average is low compared to the world's spiritual need. However, how much more could we all do, how much more time could we all lend, when you consider the number of Christians there are in America—or the world, where there are an estimated 261 million in the U.S. and more than 2.2 billion around the globe, according to *WorldData.org*.

The same 36 percent are the ones that also participate in my church's outreach ministries. With this in mind, it's worth stressing again: there is a need to give time, not only in the church, but outside of the church.

Value each granule of time, as you would the sand in an Hourglass.

TAKE A MOMENT TO FOCUS

*Read the question and
write what comes to mind.*

Are you spending your time for the right reasons, instead of just following the crowd?

_____

_____

_____

_____

_____

_____

_____

_____

_____

_____

_____

"Time is the coin of your life. It is the only coin you have, and only you can determine how it is spent.
Be careful lest you let other people spend it for you."

- Carl Sandburg

PROPER INVESTMENT OF TIME

Are you investing your time properly? Let me be more specific. Are you investing your time into the right people? How many times have you thought that someone is holding you back, for instance? (Hopefully, you are not the one holding someone else back.) Allowing ourselves to be held back is a mistake that each of us has made at some point in our lives. However, it is easier to see this mistake in others than in ourselves.

A simple fact is, there are people who require more care than others, and no matter how much we give, they seem to grow worse, not better. So, while it's true that it is always good to invest in others, the wise investor will know where to place their investments, and how to carefully monitor them, to achieve the greatest return.

Some investments require more attention than others, on the surface. Think of a mother caring for a difficult child while neglecting a child who behaves well. What do you think can happen with the well-behaved child, as a result?

My wife and I have a son with disabilities. Until recently, if we didn't place nearly all of our attention on him, he would act up to get it. Although he has disabilities, there are people without them who do the same to get attention.

Many business owners invest a large portion of their time on under-performing employees as opposed to continued training and personal growth for their best workers. If they would put some of their time into their best employees, they would likely get even better and more efficient at their jobs. Similarly, there are many pastors who burn themselves out ministering to the broken instead of training potential leaders to help shoulder the load. This is true in many other areas of leadership, too.

What can you do if you find yourself in this situation? Follow the ABC's of investing time.

Acknowledge:

Acknowledge that not only your money and energy, but also your time is a finite resource. It pays to say "yes" to the right people and opportunities. Remember, too, a "yes" to one person or situation is a "no" to someone or something else. So consider carefully and make wise decisions.

Become:

Become aware of where you are investing your time. Your calendar will reveal the truth, and this knowledge will offer tremendous insight. With a proper and honest assessment, you can determine the necessary changes.

Change:

Change your situation. You may have to end activities that are unproductive or unhealthy. You may even need to establish boundaries for certain relationships.

Relationships have a greater influence on how you invest your time than you think. **1 Corinthians 15:33 (AMPC)** says, "Do not be so deceived and misled! Evil companionships (communion, associations) corrupt and deprave good manners and morals and character."

Part of the change process is to identify activities and people to invest in.

There may be those you have overlooked who would be valuable to your success and you to theirs. When identifying these people, think about how much they represent your future. Consider, are they someone you would like to have as a mentor? Are they someone you need to mentor?

Each one of us is the best steward of our own time. Pencil these people into your calendar. Be intentional with these relationships. They could represent your legacy.

You may think this has been a bit harsh, especially when you think about your relationships that may change as a result. Yet, Jesus was sent to the earth to die for sinners. However, He spent the majority of His ministry with twelve men. There were others with them, but He was to share the secrets of the Kingdom with these twelve. Everyone else was taught only in parables.

Consider, too, that God invested time in His greatest creation: us. **Isaiah 49:16 (AMPC)** says, "Behold, I have indelibly imprinted (tattooed a picture of) you on the palm of each of My hands . . . "

Review **Genesis 1:4-31** for the work God did in each of the six days of creation. God was doing more than just creating tangible things. He was setting time itself in place with ways to measure it. The sun, stars, and moon were set in place to determine increments of time for the day. These would also assist in the measuring of time for days, weeks, months, and years.

God is an eternal Spirit and does not operate in time, but is the controller of time. He has made promises that when we obey His word, our days shall be lengthened. David said in **Psalm 39:4 (AMPC)**, "Lord, make me to know my end and [to appreciate] the measure of my days—what it is; let me know and realize how frail I am [how transient is my stay here]."

Our time here has a limit. Invest well, my friends! And always remember, when it comes to investing time in relationships, God must be priority No. 1.

TAKE A MOMENT TO FOCUS

*Read the question and
write what comes to mind.*

Are you being mentored and are you investing time in mentoring others?

_____

_____

_____

_____

_____

_____

_____

_____

_____

_____

_____

_____

_____

"Once you have experienced quality time with God, time quality will never be the same."

- Daniel Evans

In modern industrialized cultures, we often take time for granted. Even though time truly is our greatest asset, we consistently spend it with relatively little forethought, and sometimes quite unwisely. Oftentimes, this occurs with little thought or awareness of what we have done. Consider the following time-related idioms and how they help elaborate on this thought.

Note: An idiom is a figurative phrase not always taken literally. It can express a particular sentiment but does not mean what its individual words mean. As such, an idiom is a saying that is specific to a particular language and culture.

In our own language, we use these phrases daily and misuse our time and the time of others. Every second that passes draws us closer to eternity, either with regrets or rewards. So, making every second count should be the goal for each of us.

We are habitual creatures by nature, and we create habits that become second nature to us. One of these is a bad habit we practice often—a destroyer of our greatest asset—and we often give no thought to it. Simply put, we waste our time. And perhaps just as bad, we waste the time of others.

This bad habit is committed so deeply that we do not realize we are throwing our time away as we might our money. These wasting–of–time moments happen in everyday life. So the next time someone asks you to do something, pay attention to what you agree to and what impact it will have on your life and the lives of others. In addition, when you say, "Give me a second," think about what you are saying to the person who asked you for help.

Without realizing your expectations on others, you are demanding them to wait for you until you are able or ready to respond. Most wait to be courteous, but others wait because they really need the help. This is just an example to illustrate how habitual phrases can cost us all a great asset. Other idioms, as it turns out, can be even greater wasters of time.

Here's a list of commonly used American idioms that can help shine light on how our asset of time can oftentimes bear little fruit and deliver us little or no return.

1. "Better late than never" is used to acknowledge that while something may not be completed with time to spare, the task is at least now complete.

2. "Killing time" or "to kill time" often describes an interval or span of time spent idly or aimlessly.

3. "Time flies" or "time flies when you're having fun" is an expression of how quickly time passes.

4. "Wasting time" or "a waste of time" refers to spending time doing something that serves no purpose.

5. "Make up for lost time" is when someone is catching up on time gone away.

6. "It's about time" is a way to say that something should've happened a long time ago.

7. "Give me a second" or "wait a minute" means to allow you just a little more time before you move to your next task.

No matter how much we either value time or take it for granted, time is ticking. And we cannot change that fact.

These examples of various time-related idioms are not provided to point out flaws in us as individuals, but rather to bring awareness to the fact that we waste time more than we realize. It is habitual and it happens often. We check our financial accounts more than we do the greatest asset we have. My prayer is that we will not neglect what is so valuable and be better stewards of our precious time. Time is ticking!

TAKE A MOMENT TO FOCUS

*Read the question and
write what comes to mind.*

Are you considerate of the time of others?

_____

_____

_____

_____

_____

_____

_____

_____

_____

_____

_____

_____

_____

"Regret for wasted time is more wasted time."

- **Mason Cooley**

SETTING YOUR TIME STRAIGHT

Pray right now and ask God to help you be a better steward of your time. Pray this aloud!

Father in Heaven, the Master of time itself, thank you for eternal life. I know I am on earth to use my time for you and others. I repent and ask Your forgiveness for wasting any of this most valuable gift You have given me. Wash me by Jesus' blood and make my heart clean in this area. My time is ticking away. Help me to invest as much of it as possible in You and others. I desire to serve You and others with my time. Help me to prioritize You in Your rightful place in my life. Afterwards, I know everything else will fall in place. Thank You for hearing my prayer, in Jesus' name. Amen!

Now, since things are in order between you and the Lord, listen to the Holy Spirit. He will lead you into the best investments of your time. Helping people by giving them your time is the best gift you can give. It may take money and other things to help meet their needs. However, the time you invest is something that once you give it, you can never get it back. That is why the rewards will be eternal and will even carry rewards here on earth. One of the rewards on earth will be the satisfaction of knowing you have helped someone by dispensing an irreplaceable resource. In addition, you will have the knowledge that you spent and invested your time well, as Jesus would have.

Let's do some investing! After all, investing time with the return of eternal rewards is an investor's dream.

TAKE A MOMENT TO FOCUS

*Read the question and
write what comes to mind.*

What changes can you make to be a better steward of your time?

_____

_____

_____

_____

_____

_____

_____

_____

_____

_____

_____

_____

_____

"Lost time is never found again."

- Benjamin Franklin

MORE FROM DANIEL EVANS

Are you ready to learn how to be more successful and significant? Do you maintain satisfaction in the midst of growing pains? You will be able to answer these questions and more in one day.

This one-day process takes you through five steps. The practicality in the steps helps bring clarity and revelation. Dedicate one day and glean many days after.

The Five Steps

Step 1 – Stay Focused

Step 2 – Make Commitments

Step 3 – Implement Structure

Step 4 – Learn to Glean

Step 5 – Measure Up

"A Commitment to Unleash Your Leader Potential" is specifically for the leader in each of us. You may ask, "Who, me?" Yes, this includes you, as well! When you think about it, every person living is a leader. It may be in a positive or a negative way, but you lead others by influencing them.

You influence somebody, sometime, somewhere, in some way. I call this "The Four Areas of Leadership Influence."

You may say, "Alright, you have my attention. Where do we go from here?"

First, you must identify your four areas. You will then have clarity on your strengths. Weaknesses will surface, as well. This will allow you to maximize your "some ways" for a positive impact.

Personal growth is very important and does not come overnight. Many try to grow too quickly, and they miss so much value due to impatience. It is like

telephone poles you can count from a car. However, from a speeding train they appear more like a picket fence.

Invest Well!

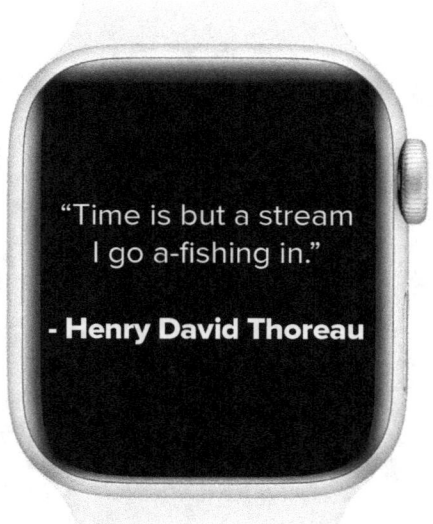

"Time is but a stream
I go a-fishing in."

- Henry David Thoreau

www.ingramcontent.com/pod-product-compliance
Lightning Source LLC
Chambersburg PA
CBHW061323120626
46546CB00007B/2659

9 7 8 1 9 6 1 6 1 4 0 4 8